by Lisa Eisenberg & Katy Hall

Illustrated by Don Orehek

SCHOLASTIC INC.
New York Toronto London Auckland Sydney

To the classiest kids in any class:
Leigh, Kate, and Annie.

ISBN 0-590-41182-9

48 47 46 45 44 43 42 41 40 6 7 8/0

Printed in the U.S.A. 01

First Scholastic printing, September 1987

101
SCHOOL
JOKES

CLASSROOM CRACK-UPS

What furniture polish do schools use?

Pledge of Allegiance.

Why do teachers take aspirin?

For de-tension headaches.

Who's your best friend at school?

Your princi-pal.

What does everyone at school do at the same time?

Grow older.

How do messy students write their reports?

With their pigpens.

What did one arithmetic book say to the other?

I really have a lot of problems.

BUS STOPPERS

Jim: Why don't you take the bus home?

Ted: I can't. My mother would make me bring it back.

Bus Driver: Steffie, look outside and see if the turn signal is on.

Steffie: Yes-no-yes-no-yes-no. . . .

Policeman: Didn't you see that sign saying "one way"?

Bus Driver: But, Officer, I'm only going one way.

Why did they bury the school bus?

The battery was dead, the pistons were shot, and then the engine died.

Who can hold up a school bus with only one hand?

A policeman.

What happens to a student who misses the last school bus?

He catches it when he gets home.

CLASS CLOWN

Why did the class clown spend the whole night crawling around on the playground?

He'd lost his marbles.

Why did the class clown take her computer to school?

Her mom told her to bring in an apple for the teacher.

Why did the class clown give Jenny a dog biscuit?

He heard she was the teacher's pet.

ALDO
DOG
BISCUIT

Why did the class clown throw a bucket of water off the top of the school?

He wanted to make a big splash in front of his class.

Why wouldn't the class clown use hair oil the night before the big test?

He didn't want anything to slip his mind.

Why did the class clown ask the music teacher for a B-flat?

She wanted to take a note home to her mother.

Why did the class clown eat the dollar he brought to school?

It was his lunch money.

TEACHER FEATURES

Teacher: Ralph, if you can't tell me where the Appalachians are, I'm going to keep you after school.
Ralph: But I didn't take them.

Principal: Will you pass the nuts?
Teacher: No, I think I'll flunk them.

Teacher: Sally, do you thirst after knowledge?

Sally: No, I thirst after salted peanuts.

Teacher: Has anyone here ever seen the Catskill Mountains?

Ed: No, but I've seen the cats kill mice.

Why are kindergarten teachers so good?

They know how to make little things count.

TV SCHOOL GUIDE

9:00	Tardy Boys Mystery
10:00	Pupils' Court
11:00	National Ice Hookey Play-offs
12:00	Lunch Hour of Power
1:00	Dunce Fever
2:00	Flunky Brewster
3:00	The A-plus Team
4:00	The Fail Guy
5:00	Stay After School Special

Jill: Mom, the teacher says I have to write more clearly.
Mom: That's a good idea.
Jill: No, it isn't. Then she'll know I can't spell.

Mom: Freddy's teacher says he needs an encyclopedia.
Pop: Encyclopedia my eye! Let him walk to school the way I did.

Pop: Max, how did you do on your history test?

Max: Not so good. They asked me about things that happened before I was born.

Mom: Don't you think there should be a club for kids at school?

Pop: Only when kindness fails.

Father: How were your test scores, Son?

Son: Underwater, Dad.

Father: What do you mean, underwater?

Son: You know, below C level.

TIMES

Fran: Dad, can you help me find the least common denominator?

Dad: Good heavens, girl! Haven't they found that yet?

THE LUNCH BUNCH

Knock, knock!
Who's there?
Dewey.
Dewey who?
Dewey have to eat all these beets?

Knock, knock!
Who's there?
Juicy.
Juicy who?
Juicy any extra desserts over here?

Knock, knock!

Who's there?

Roxanne.

Roxanne who?

Roxanne pebbles are in this meatloaf!

Knock, knock!
Who's there?
Eileen.
Eileen who?
Eileen over to slurp my soup.

Knock, knock!
Who's there?
Philip.
Philip who?
Philip my glass, please.

Knock, knock!
Who's there?
Felix.
Felix who?
Felix my ice cream, I'll lick his!

Knock, knock!
Who's there?
Duncan.
Duncan who?
Duncan doughnuts in your milk
makes them soggy.

DAFFY-NITIONS

Writer's Cramp: What kids develop when it's time to do their homework.

Declaration of Independence: A note excusing you from school.

A Smarty Pants: A kid who carries a dictionary in her pocket.

TABLE TALK

"The hot dogs aren't bad," Sam said frankly.

"I can't eat these red peppers," Pam said hotly.

"Please pass the sugar," Lee said sweetly.

"I'll have a soda," Bea said coaxingly.

"This lemon soda tastes bad!" Beth said bitterly.

"Pass the pumpernickel," Seth said wryly.

"This milk is too cold," Juan said icily.

"Best pancakes I ever had!" Dawn said flatly.

"This soup is boiling!" Greg said heatedly.

"My soup is freezing," Meg said coldly.

"I spilled my milk," Donny said moistly.

"I have chunky peanut butter," Lonny said smoothly.

"No more pickles for me!" Ronny said sourly.

"This bread is fresh, for a change," Bonnie said softly.

"This meat's too well-done," Andy said dryly.

"There's onion on this sandwich!" Mandy said sharply.

"These string beans are overcooked," Randy said limply.

MATH MADNESS

Teacher: How many sides does a square box have?

Dan: Two. The inside and the outside.

Teacher: If you add 399, 60, 21, 75, and 600, what would you get?

Ann: The wrong answer.

Teacher: Ted, if your father had ten dollars and you asked him for six dollars, how many dollars would your father have left?

Ted: Ten.

Teacher: You don't know your math.

Ted: You don't know my father.

What classroom table doesn't have any legs?

The multiplication table.

Diane: Which is correct — five plus four is eleven, or five plus four are eleven?

Teacher: Neither. Five plus four is nine.

HYSTERICAL HISTORY

Teacher: Who can tell me why Robin Hood robbed the rich?
Steve: Because the poor didn't have any money.

Teacher: The former ruler of Russia was called the czar, and his wife was the czarina. Who can tell me what his children were called?
David: Czardines.

Teacher: Who can tell me when the Iron Age ended?

Ann: When drip-dry clothes were invented.

Why didn't Alex want to study history?

He thought it was better to let bygones be bygones.

WHO WAS THE 32nd PRESIDENT OF THE UNITED STATES?

Teacher: Lisa, when was the Great Depression?

Lisa: Last week when I got my report card.

THE LUNCH BUNCH AGAIN

Knock, knock!
Who's there?
Imus.
Imus who?
Imus get out of this cafeteria!

Knock, knock!
Who's there?
Ketchup.
Ketchup who?
Ketchup with her before she leaves!

WEIRD SCIENCE

Teacher: Tim, what do you know about shooting stars?
Tim: No comet.

Teacher: Gus, name a deadly poison.
Gus: Aviation.
Teacher: That's not right.
Gus: Well, one drop is sure to kill you.

Teacher: Why did Irving disconnect the doorbell?
Julius: He wanted to win the no-bell prize.

Teacher: What happens when the human body is completely submerged in water?
Debbie: The telephone rings.

Todays lesson
Animals of the
Arctic region

Teacher: Name six animals of the Arctic region.

Ted: Three walruses and three polar bears.

MORE CLASSROOM CRACK-UPS

When are kids most likely to go into school?

When the door is open.

What kind of test do kids find most painful?

A blood test.

What tree do you find in every grade school?

The elemen-tree.

What do you call that great feeling you get when you finish your arithmetic homework?

The aftermath.

What candy do kids like to eat on the playground?

Recess Pieces.

What happened when the principal fell into the copying machine?

She was beside herself.

COPYING MACHINE

WHIZ KIDS

Teacher: How do you spell Mississippi?
George: The state or the river?

Teacher: Who was Karl Marx?
Gail: One of the Marx brothers.

Teacher: What is the first part of a geography book?
Alice: The table of continents.

Teacher: Edna, name two pronouns.
Edna: Who me?
Teacher: Right.

Teacher: Who can tell me where the English Channel is?

Jane: I don't know. It's not on my TV.

Coach: Send in a new pitcher!
Catcher: What a relief.

Coach: Why did you bring your math homework to exercise class?
Bonnie: I have to reduce some fractions.

Coach: What's the first step in saving a person who's drowning?
Walter: Take him out of the water.
Coach: What's the second step?
Walter: Take the water out of him.

Coach: Swimming is one of the best ways to keep your body slim and trim.
Alice: That's funny. I've never seen a slim, trim whale.

COACH
8

What do you call a kid who plays basketball in a shirt and tie?

A gym dandy.

Phyllis: Coach, is this water healthy for swimming?
Coach: Absolutely! It's well water.

What color is a cheerleader?

Yeller.

Does it take longer to run from first base to second or from second base to third?

From second to third, because there's a short stop in the middle.

Donny: I have a chance at the baseball team.
Lonny: Are they raffling it off?

Lolly: Whew! It's a hot day for a football game.

Molly: Yeah, let's go sit in front of Polly. She's a big fan.

What insect does well in school?

The spelling bee.

What subject do snakes like?

Hiss-*tory.*

What subject do mosquitoes like?

Ar-itch-metic.

What subject do witches like?

Spelling.

What school did Sir Lancelot go to?

Knight school.

Why do werewolves do well in school?

They give snappy answers.

Why didn't the skeleton want to go to school?

His heart wasn't in it.

What kind of school do you have to drop out of to graduate?

Parachute school.

In what school do you learn how to greet people?

Hi school.

In what school do you learn how to write good letters?

Correspondence school.

Where do soda jerks go to school?

Sundae school.

What do you call a student whose library books are overdue?

A bookkeeper.

When fish swim in schools, who helps out the teacher?

The herring aid.

Why do some kids forget to come to school?

They're absent-*minded.*

Why did the one-thousand-year-old Egyptian join the PTA?

He heard it was for mummies and daddies!

What can you draw without crayons?

Your breath.

What did the pencil say to the paper?

I dot my i's on you.

What kind of paper makes you itch?

Scratch paper.

Jim: Do you like homework?
Tim: I like NOTHING better.

What's all over the school building?

The roof.

Ann: Hurray! The teacher said we'd have a test today, rain or shine.

Dan: Then why are you so happy?

Ann: It's snowing.

What room can a student never enter?

A mushroom.

Peggy: What did I make in arithmetic?
Teacher: Mistakes.

How can you tell if a school is haunted?

If it has a school spirit.

FIRST AID FUNNIES

School Nurse: Danny, what did the doctor find when she examined the X ray of your head?

Danny: Nothing.

School Nurse: Your cough sounds better today.

Ellen: It should. I practiced all night.

School Nurse: What happened to your nose? It's totally flat.

Dick: My teacher told me to keep it to the grindstone.

SCHOOL
NURSE

School Secretary: You say Ernie has a bad cold and can't come to school? Who is this speaking?

Voice on Telephone: This is my father.

What's the best way to get to the nurse's office?

Fall off the jungle gym.

THE LAST OF THE LUNCH BUNCH

Knock, knock!
Who's there?
Goat!
Goat who?
Goat tell the principal that this food stinks.

Knock, knock!
Who's there?
Isabel.
Isabel who?
Isabel ringing for lunch?

Knock, knock!

Who's there?

Henrietta.

Henrietta who?

Henrietta worm that was in his apple!

Knock, knock!
Who's there?
Annie.
Annie who?
Annie body ready to eat?

Knock, knock!
Who's there?
Howard.
Howard who?
Howard you like half of my marshmallow-mustard sandwich?

Knock, knock!
Who's there?
Ammonia.
Ammonia who?
Ammonia little bit hungry.

Dick: There's a spider on my salad.
Cafeteria Cook: Sorry, I didn't know you were a vegetarian.

TODAY'S
MENU
MILK

JUST TESTING

School Psychologist: What brings you to my office?

Student: I think I'm a dog!

School Psychologist: Well, let's talk about it. Why don't you lie down on my couch?

Student: I can't! I'm not allowed on the furniture!

Student: Doctor, I think I'm a bullfrog.

School Psychologist: Hmmm, how long have you thought that?

Student: Ever since I was a little tadpole!

SCHOOL
PSYCHOLOGIST

Student: You've got to help me! I'm starting to believe I'm a pretzel!

School Psychologist: Well, come into my office and I'll see if I can straighten you out.

READ-ICULOUS!

How to Succeed in School
by Rita Book

Make Your Teacher Happy
by Sid Down

Speaking in Front of the School
by Audie Torium

Special Moments Outside Class
by Rhea Cess

Make Your Teacher Mad
by Stan Dupp

What I Did Last Summer
by Fay Cation

I Slept While Teacher Wrote
by Chuck Bored

Getting Ready for Vacation
by Anita Break

FINALS!

Why did Ralph's teacher give him a B?

He had hives.

Why do students get a lot of exercise?

They're always pursuing their studies.

POP
CORN

When is corn like a little quiz?

When it's popped.

How do you get a rest during gym class?

Sit down on one of the laps.

When is a boring lesson like a broken pencil?

When it has no point.

What's the hardest part about taking a test?

The answers.